Uncluttered

Shaping Your Heart & Home
for What Matters Most

A 28-Day Devotional
By Liana George & Angie Hyche

scrivinspire

To those who feel overwhelmed by all the chaos and clutter, Hope is here.

table of contents

introduction

How to Use the Uncluttered Devotional

Welcome to *Uncluttered*! Our prayer is that this four-week devotional will inspire you, both spiritually and practically, in your mission to unclutter and shape your life for what matters most.

Whether you aim to declutter your spaces, streamline your schedule, or clear your mind, each devotional provides snippets of encouragement to help you achieve success and understand God's view on various organizing principles.

The subsequent prayers are simply a starting point for you. Spending time in prayer throughout this process will enable you to grow even closer to God and to hear the voice of God's Spirit guiding you along the way.

The sections titled "Now, Unclutter It!" are hands-on and/or reflective challenges that can help you apply the ideas highlighted within the devotional. While you may be tempted to skip these activities, we highly suggest you try them out and see how they can impact your efforts. Of course, we know some of them will take longer to complete than others, but don't feel like you must do everything all at once.

You may choose to work through all the material in 28 days straight, spend one day on the devotional and one day on the application, or give yourself a week (or more) to complete each day.

Just like with organizing, there is no one-size-fits-all as to how you approach the material. You do you!

Finally, there's a reflections page for you to jot down your thoughts about that day's topic or to complete the Unclutter It! activities.

It's our hope that *Uncluttered* will be a useful and constant resource on your organizing journey. We're confident that these devotions will not only help you bring order to your life but will also allow you to see the connection between faith and organized living. God wants that for you and so do we.

Here's to becoming uncluttered together!

day 1

The God of Order

"For God is not a God of disorder, but of peace."
1 Corinthians 14:33 (NIV)

How well do you know God? Who do you say that He is?

From Sunday School lessons to powerful sermons at church, you've probably heard descriptions of who God is—God the Creator, the Great I Am, the Lord Who Provides, and the Lord Who Sees. We're also told in Scripture that His character is loving, merciful, and kind, among other things.

But have you ever stopped to consider God as a God of Order?

To be honest, I hadn't. Until I reread Genesis 1:2, "Now the earth was formless and void ..." According to the original text, the terms formless and void were meant to convey the idea of confusion and disorder. God took that chaos and set the universe in order. From there, everything He did in Scripture (and still does today) is done in an organized manner. That's His character. His nature. That's who He is.

And He wants us, His children, to be a reflection of that order too.

As God's image-bearers (Genesis 1:27), we were created to resemble, or be a representative of, Him on the earth. The world should be able to see the characteristics of God through us and our

1

everyday actions. This includes the way we manage and organize our homes, our time, and other aspects of our lives.

Tall orders, right? Take heart. As we learn to be patient and wise, we can grow in our ability to be organized as well.

And though we will never be able to perfectly emulate God's nature in full, understanding who He is and what He longs for us to be can help us work toward becoming better reflections of His character to a world that desperately needs to see Him.

God, the God of Order. Just as He establishes order in the heights of heaven (Job 25:2), let's do our part to reflect His nature and that majesty here on earth.

Liana

prayer

Father God, I praise You for who You are,
a God of Order.
You create order in the heavens above and the earth below.
Help me to reflect Your organized nature,
so that others might see and
know You.

God's orderly attributes

Have you ever stopped and thought about God and the way in which He operates in an organized fashion? While you may have read the Bible numerous times, His organized ways may not have been on your radar. But for us to be His image-bearers, we need to see for ourselves exactly how God functions!

Look up the following verses and record how God displays order/orderly principles:

- Genesis 1:1-31
- Jeremiah 29:11, Psalm 33:11, Ephesians 2:10
- Genesis 2:19
- Genesis 6:14-22, Exodus 25-30

Can you think of any other passages of Scripture that show God's organized nature?

reflection:

How are you more aware of who God is after looking up these verses? How does it encourage your heart or spur you to action?

Reflections

day 2

Am I A Good Steward?

"Every good and perfect gift is from above."
James 1:17 (NIV)

Several years ago, I was surprised to discover two large dust-covered bins filled with quilts and blankets in our attic. But these weren't just run-of-the-mill linens. They had been lovingly handmade by my husband's mother and grandmothers to celebrate special occasions.

I'm ashamed to confess I had forgotten them.

Brushing my fingers across each one, I thought about the hours spent planning, choosing materials, and sewing. How could I have let these beautiful pieces of art be consigned to years of oblivion in a gloomy attic?

To honor them, I made the conscious decision to either use them or let them go. I set to work, determined that each treasure would serve a purpose. While a few were donated, I was able to use several as bedspreads and displayed the others. Finally, they were all being enjoyed.

When we consider the possessions we own, we need to remember they aren't really ours. They are all God-given. We are His stewards of them.

Steward is an uncommon word but a familiar concept. In biblical times, a steward acted like a manager, who was responsible for overseeing a home. Since stewards didn't own the home or its contents, they acted in the best interest of their master.

Understanding this principle can help us apply a new standard to our possessions. Are we treating our belongings with care so they will last? Are we using them in a way that glorifies God and serves others?

Armed with this knowledge, how would you judge your stewardship of all that God has blessed you with? Could items currently stored in your attic, basement, and closets be used, displayed, or donated?

Just as my mother-in-law would beam with pleasure at the thought of her quilts being used, when you make the changes required to be a better steward, you can be content knowing your belongings are utilized as God intended.

Angie

prayer

Father, thank You for Your good gifts, including my physical
belongings.
You've given me all I need and more.
I recognize that all I have is from You and belongs to You.
Show me how I can best care for my belongings.
Give me a spirit of stewardship with the wisdom to use them in a way
that glorifies You.

stewardship home tour

As Christians, we know that everything we have is from God, and we are simply stewards, tasked with the responsibility of using our belongings in a way that glorifies Him. With that principle in mind, it's time for a brief home tour.

1. Grab some paper and a pen or pencil, and take 5-10 minutes to walk around your home. You don't have to tour your entire home. Just visit a few places where a lot of items are stored, such as a basement, garage, attic, or a large closet. Without taking the time to open containers and sort through individual items, write down some categories of items you see. Examples might include seasonal decor, craft supplies, collectibles, clothing, sports equipment, or dishes.

2. Read the following Scriptures and jot down a few notes about the verses.

    a. Psalm 24:1
    b. Proverbs 3:9
    c. 1 Timothy 6:17-19

3. Consider what you saw on your tour in light of the above Scriptures. Ask God to show you how to honor Him with the belongings He has entrusted to you.

4. Write down any insights from your prayer and study time.

reflection:

How have you used your home to serve God? How might you be able to do so more or in a new way once you've decluttered?

Reflections

day 3

Are You Observing the
Warning Signs?

*"A prudent man sees danger and takes refuge,
but the simple keep going and suffer for it."*
Proverbs 22:3 (NIV)

Zoom! A speeding red vehicle rushed past me on the highway. I craned my neck to find the source of all the commotion. Eyeing a cherry-colored Porsche attempting to bypass those of us who waited in line, I shook my head. *Which of the orange signs a mile back did the driver not see? How did he miss the flashing lights indicating an upcoming lane change?* In doing so, this NASCAR speedster created more traffic issues, slowing everyone down, and inciting unnecessary road rage.

Don't get me wrong; I'm all too guilty of using this tactic myself when I've been in a hurry! But when I behave this way and try to justify my actions, I only cause trouble for myself and for those around me. It's not good.

And it's eerily similar to what many of my organizing clients have shared with me, *"I know I have too much stuff and should declutter and organize, but I don't."* Then, they proceed to rattle off a long list of excuses that keep them mired down in the chaos and clutter. Like the reckless Porsche owner, they see the signs, choose not to do anything, and ultimately suffer for it. Usually at the expense of their physical health, their mental stability, or their relationships.

But not every disorganized person acts that way. Many see the mess that has crept in, understand the effects it has on their lives, and proceed to do whatever it takes to stop the madness around them. By seeking refuge in a more organized lifestyle, they gain the peace and contentment their choices provide.

Are the warning signs of a disorderly life flashing in front of you? Standing at the crossroads, you have a decision to make: will you acknowledge the warning signs and bring positive results to your home and life? Or will you ignore them, choosing to stay in the chaos and suffering for it?

Ultimately, the choice is yours.

Liana

prayer

Father, help me see and heed the warning signs You're flashing in front of me.
Provide me with Your strength so I can implement the necessary steps to bring order to my spaces and so I can have the peace and contentment that You offer.
Above all else, I want to be a prudent person, not a foolish one.

danger signs

Can you see the danger in front of you?

While there's probably no large billboard flashing in your house, telling you that your clutter is causing you harm, there may be subtle signs that things are off. But how can you know what they are so you can course correct?

Here are a few indicators that trouble is on the horizon, and you might want to take action:

- You can't close your drawers or find things easily in them because there's too much stuff
- Your family members are too embarrassed to invite friends over because of the condition of your house
- You are mentally and physically spent from having too many activities on your calendar
- Others are encouraging you to seek help or threatening to leave if things don't improve
- Your finances are in a perilous state because you keep spending money on things you already own but can't find, or you're behind on payments because you're too disorganized to pay your bills on time

Other warning signs flashing in front of me:

_____

_____

_____

Once you've identified the warning signs, choose one to focus on, then take the necessary steps to fix it. What do you need to do to bring things back to normal and remove the risks to your well-being?

reflection:

Why have you been ignoring the warning signs and how has that affected you, your loved ones, and your life? How can knowing the warning signs make a difference moving forward?

Reflections

day 4

Traveling Light

"For this world is not our permanent home;
we are looking forward to a home yet to come."
Hebrews 13:14 (NLT)

I'm a travel packrat. When I set out on a trip, my suitcases are often filled with extra clothes, shoes, and other items I don't really need. With so much weighing me down, I'm oftentimes forced to check my bags ($$), and I don't leave room for any souvenirs I might want to purchase on my getaway. I've also found it to be physically challenging to carry large pieces of luggage from one location to the next.

It's taken a lot of flights, bus rides, and train trips to discover the error of my ways and embrace the concept of journeying with less. It's a lesson I'm embracing, not only for my globe-trotting ways, but for my heart and house as well.

As Christians, this earth is not our final landing spot. We are simply travelers passing through on our way to our eternal destination —Heaven. Yet, if we aren't careful, we can overpack our lives so much that we lose sight of what and who matters most on the trek. Too many items clogging up our closets, cabinets, and calendars can indicate our baggage is tilting the scales in an unfavorable direction, leaving us financially, emotionally, physically, and relationally depleted. Definitely not the "life to the fullest" Jesus offers.

Is your schedule so full you don't have time to visit with someone who needs companionship? Are you in a constant state of anxiety from all the clutter in your house? Do you spend more money than you should because you can't find items you know you already own? If so, you might want to spend some time repacking your suitcase.

In Psalm 39:5, the psalmist reminds us our lives are but a breath. A vapor that vanishes, a puff of air. Whether your time on this earth is a short getaway or an extended vacation, you need to pack properly for the journey. Not too much. Not too little. Only what is essential for the trip.

Liana

prayer

Day 4

Father, thank You for this life You've given us.
As we travel toward our eternal home,
may we not be heavy-laden with the things of this world,
but encourage our hearts to travel light.
For when we do, the journey is a much fuller experience.

bon voyage, clutter

If you want to embrace less in your life, the best way to start is to send your clutter packing. But we know that's not an easy task, so we want to make it fun.

For this Unclutter It, you'll be writing a breakup letter to your clutter (think Dear John). Feel free to pour out all your emotions in this letter —from how it makes you feel, the problems it's caused you, and what you hope to gain by severing this relationship. Finally, make a declaration that you are done with your clutter and that you will not be getting back together.

Here's a prompt to get you started:

Dear Clutter,

> *We need to talk.*

> *We've been together for a really long time. But I've come to the realization that this "thing" we've got going on isn't really working for me.*

> *I think it's time we broke up.*

Once you've finished writing your letter, place it somewhere visible so you can be reminded that you no longer have a relationship with clutter. Then, allow yourself the time and emotions of a breakup. After that, you're ready to start afresh!

reflection:

How did it feel to break up with your clutter? What did you discover by doing this activity?

Reflections

day 5

Just in Case

"So don't worry about these things, saying, 'What will we eat? What will we drink? What will we wear?'...
Seek the Kingdom of God above all else, and live righteously, and he will give you everything you need."
Matthew 6:31, 33 (NLT)

Just in case. Three little words with a lot of power.

Of all the reasons we struggle to let things go, keeping something "just in case" reigns supreme.

There are several levels of just-in-case decisions, from the practical to the seemingly ridiculous. "I'll keep this umbrella just in case it rains" is worlds away from "I'll keep a three-month supply of food and water just in case of a zombie apocalypse." The first situation is believable, while the second is more akin to the plot of a horror movie than to reality.

Most decluttering decisions fall somewhere between the two.

Why is this so difficult? Sometimes, we don't take the time to evaluate the odds of needing the item in the future. Or we fail to consider what would be required in terms of effort or money if we let it go, only to need it later. Often, simply mulling over these two questions yields the information we need to make a good decision.

On a deeper level, the obstacle is a lack of trust. If we release the object in question, what will happen? Will we regret, suffer needlessly, and internally kick ourselves for making a poor choice? And the ultimate question—will God come through for us? Can we trust Him to take care of us?

Matthew 6 gives us all the assurance we need. How comforting to know that if we put God first, He'll take care of us! What if you and I made a conscious decision to put Him to the test? What if we put our faith in God's promise?

I don't know about you, but I refuse to keep an unnecessary stockpile. I'm going to trust that God will provide. Is there some risk involved? Maybe. Will it be worth it? Absolutely. I can't wait to see how God will work.

Angie

prayer

Day 5

Heavenly Father, I confess that I've not always
trusted You to take care of me.
I've kept many things I don't need because of fear.
I resolve to trust You to provide for me when I let go
of those things I've kept "just in case."
Thank You for being a faithful promise-keeper.

worst-case scenario

Oh, how we worry. Both the trivial and the tragic trip us up in our decluttering efforts.

At times, we may find it helpful to consider what would occur if the proverbial worst-case scenario actually happened. Going down that road mentally can shed some light on how we would handle the consequences. We may discover that it really wouldn't be as bad as we feared. This knowledge, in addition to God's promises in passages like Matthew 6:25-34, just might motivate us to shed more freely. And we may sense God's blessing as we act in faith.

Complete the following exercise:

• Summarize Matthew 6:25-34 in your own words.

• Pray for God's guidance and wisdom.

• List 3-5 items or categories of items you've kept "just in case." A few may come to mind immediately, but it might take a few minutes to think of the others. You might need to walk around your home or talk to others who share your home.

- For each one, consider:

  o How likely are you to need this item in the future?
  o What would happen if you got rid of something but then
  needed it later?
  o Does someone you know well have the same item or
  something similar you could borrow?
  o Do you have something else that could accomplish the same
  purpose?
  o If you had to buy it again, how much time and money
  would it take to get it?
  o If you needed an item but couldn't easily replace it, what's
  the worst that could happen?

- Keeping in mind the Scripture and answers to these questions, make
a decision about each item.

reflection:

How did this exercise help you understand your tendency to keep
things "just in case"? What did you learn about yourself by completing
this exercise? How could you use these questions in the future?

Reflections

day 6

Bigger Isn't Always Better

"Do not despise these small beginnings, for the Lord rejoices to see the work begin ..."
Zechariah 4:10 (NLT)

When an author writes a novel, she doesn't complete it all at once; she writes one word, then one sentence, then a chapter, and repeats the pattern until she has a finished manuscript. A painter doesn't create a masterpiece in one setting; he starts one small brushstroke at a time until his creation is done.

In today's world, it can be hard to embrace small beginnings when we are constantly bombarded with messages of "Go big or go home" and "The bigger the better." With whatever project we're working on, we generally (and falsely) believe it has to be done all at once or that we must make a huge impact right away if we truly want to make a difference.

But in God's economy, that's not the way it works. In the Bible, things are usually upside down to what the world values. That's because God doesn't despise those first small steps.

And neither should we.

I'll admit I've been guilty, on too many occasions, of loathing the snail's pace at which a project moves. I'm a doer, a take-action kind of girl, a let's-get-it-done-now person. I don't relish in the small steps I'm taking or the foundation that I'm laying. But I should. Because in those tiny actions, I'm building muscles and routines that will benefit me later, and in other ways.

If you've become agitated by the microscopic efforts you've taken toward getting organized, don't be! Maybe just admitting you have a clutter issue is the first step you need to take before you can really start decluttering. Or perhaps you need to simply set aside some dedicated time to begin your project instead of trying to fit it into your schedule. Whatever it is, don't despise small beginnings. In time, they will build upon each other and have a major impact toward the disorder you're facing.

While small may be underrated, overlooked, and shunned by the world, take comfort in knowing that God sees you and your tiny beginnings, and He's cheering you on each step of the way.

Liana

prayer

Day 6

Lord, forgive me for despising my small beginnings.
Help me to embrace the tiny efforts I'm making and
know that they are pleasing in Your sight.
More importantly, let me not see things as the world
sees them but allow me to take comfort that Your ways are the best.

baby steps

Starting your organizing journey can be a bit overwhelming. To the point where you shut down completely and do nothing.

Rather than become paralyzed by all that getting organized entails, why not take some baby steps to move you in the right direction?

Here are a few small tasks to get you going. Ideally, you could begin with one or two and build from there. When you do, you'll find you're well on your way!

- Mark out time in your calendar (30 minutes or less per session) to spend organizing.
- Arrange for childcare if needed.
- Gather supplies you might need (decluttering signs, trash bags, donation boxes, etc.).
- Choose one space to focus on.
- Ask for help (either a friend or a professional).
- Make it fun—add music if you'd like!
- Set a timer for your designated work time.
- Work for your allotted time, then repeat as time allows.

While these may not seem like big enough steps to make a dent in your disorder, they are the first (and possibly the most important) steps you need to take. With them, you're well on your way to the orderly life you long for.

reflection:

How do small tasks and baby steps contribute to overcoming the feeling of being overwhelmed? What other small steps could you incorporate into your organizing routine?

Reflections

day 7

The Comparison Game

"Don't compare yourself with others. Just look at your own work to see if you have done anything to be proud of."
Galatians 6:4 (ERV)

My friend Flo amazes me. In addition to being smart and nice, she's also very adventurous, which is what I love most about her. While I don't spend much time with her, we stay connected through social media, where I often see what part of the world she's currently exploring. One day, she's in Wyoming, enjoying the majesty of the Tetons; the following week, she's volunteering at a bird sanctuary in South America; and the next, she's visiting family and friends in Europe.

I'm not going to lie … her nomadic lifestyle causes that ugly green monster (a.k.a. jealousy) in me to come out.

Even though I travel quite a bit and have seen a lot of the world as a former expat, I ache for her wanderlust. Then the questions start pouring out: *Why can't I be like her? Why does she get to do all those things while I don't?* And on and on they go.

The comparison game can be vicious. If left undetected, it can rob me of my joy and cause me to feel inadequate and ungrateful for the blessings I have.

Sadly, comparing ourselves to others isn't the only game we play. I witnessed it when I was helping clients with their organizing efforts. They would spend hours bringing order to their lives only to finish and compare it with the pictures they saw on Pinterest, Instagram, or Facebook. If they weren't judging their results by the images they saw there, then they'd measure themselves against the magazines and TV shows that offered a perfectly organized home setting.

When they didn't match up to the world's standards, those clients would become depressed and defeated rather than feel proud of the hard work they had put in and what they had accomplished.

At some point, we all find ourselves playing some type of comparison game. If you're caught in that trap, please know that the playing field is not level, and you'll never measure up to the staged and photoshopped images you're likening your organizing efforts to.

At the cross, however, it's all equal. That's where our focus should be. On God and what He thinks of our work. So, the next time you finish a project, don't look to the world for approval. Look to the Lord. Then, feel free to pat yourself on the back. You're one step closer to an uncluttered life!

Liana

prayer

Day 7

Lord, comparison is the thief of my joy.
Help me to see when I am starting to play
the comparison game, and may Your Spirit
stop me from continuing in the pursuit.
Set my eyes on what I'm doing and what
I've accomplished, that it may be pleasing
and honoring to You.

compare no more!

In order to stop playing the comparison game, we have to take a look at what we've been comparing ourselves and our efforts to in the past. Use these questions to help get you started:

- What do I compare my organizing efforts to? Be specific.
- How does it make me feel when I compare my results to others?
- What can I do to stop participating in the game or from being tempted in the first place?
- How can I 'pat myself on the back' for what I've accomplished?
- How do I feel when I limit my focus on my efforts and my accomplishments?

Spend some time reflecting on your answers on the reflections page provided. When you're done, commit to compare no more!

reflection:

How do your answers encourage you to stop comparing yourself and your efforts? What will you do differently moving forward?

Reflections

day 8

Be Careful How You Speak

"Do not let any unwholesome talk come out of your mouths ... "
Ephesians 4:29 (NIV)

During Christmas breaks from school, I loved curling up near a crackling fire and reading for long periods of time. My younger brother, however, would be glued to the TV, watching his favorite holiday film, *A Christmas Story*. On occasion, I'd join him on the couch and allow myself to get lost in the hilarious tale of Ralphie, a young boy obsessed with receiving a Red Ryder BB gun for Christmas.

I always squirmed at the scene where Ralphie uses a "dirty" word and has to wash his mouth with soap. Every time I saw that rust-colored bar poking out of Ralphie's mouth, I could feel flakes of the abrasive cleanser wedging themselves between my teeth, the soap slime settling on my tongue, and my saliva mixing with the large chunk to form tiny bubbles that would eventually float to the deep recesses of my throat.

Yuck!!

While I've never sucked on soap for *using* foul language, that doesn't mean I haven't *heard* it. As an organizer, my clients often uttered words that, like profanity, didn't serve them well as they worked to bring order to their lives. After hearing these negative phrases repeatedly, I began to refer to them as the "dirty" words of organizing:

Someday/Later—"I'll get to that pile of clutter someday/later."

Just in case—"I can't get rid of that; I might need it someday, so I'll hold onto it just in case."

I don't know—"I don't know where this item belongs, so I'll just put it anywhere."

I can't—"I can't get organized; it's not in my DNA."

Sound familiar? Although the words and phrases may seem harmless at first, they're actually quite dangerous. When we say them, not only do we limit our beliefs about getting organized, but we limit our ability as well.

That's because words have power.

The dirty words of organizing can leave you surrounded in chaos and clutter, while reframing your language can offer peace and life change. Which will you speak today?

Liana

prayer

Father, Scripture tells me that my words have
the power of life and death.
May the words of my mouth and the
meditations of my heart be pleasing to You
so they don't limit my beliefs or my actions.
Help me to speak truth and life that will serve me well.

what say you?

As we learned, words have tremendous power. Positive words can build us up, while negative ones can keep us stuck in the mire and mess.

In order to conquer our clutter, it's important to know the "dirty" language we're speaking when it comes to getting organized, why we're saying it, and what other words we could be using. Complete this short activity to see the impact your words are having and find new ones to empower you.

Feel free to use the words or phrases from the devotional to get you started, but consider adding some of your own too.

my "dirty" words

_____
_____
_____

what i'm really saying

_____
_____

_____

what i need to say instead

_____
_____
_____

reflection:

How have your words impacted your efforts to get organized? How can understanding their power make a difference for you?

Reflections

day 9

Constant Craving

"Enjoy what you have rather than desiring what you don't have.
Just dreaming about nice things is meaningless—like chasing the wind."
Ecclesiastes 6:9 (NLT)

Bacon cheeseburgers. Diet lemonade. Endless cups of crushed ice.

These foods represent cravings I've experienced. The first two occurred during pregnancy. The third (ice) was a symptom of iron-deficiency anemia during my college years. While cravings are sometimes related to a nutrient deficiency, others are simply expressions of ambiguous yearning.

We all know what it feels like to crave something, be it food, belongings, or prestige. God understands our longings—He made us! Lysa Terkeurst explains it well in her *Made to Crave Devotional*: "God made us to crave—to desire eagerly, want greatly, and long for Him. But Satan wants to do everything possible to replace our craving for God with something else." Inevitably these replacements leave us unsatisfied.

Choices have consequences, so our substitutes can damage us. The ice cream and potato chips I eat when I'm not hungry cause excess weight and its complications. The clothes I don't need clutter my closet. The leadership position I accept in my search for significance takes time from my family and causes me undue stress.

How do we recognize these cravings for what they really are—a longing for closeness with God? How do we overcome our continual lust for more?

Make no doubt about it, this is spiritual warfare. A battle for our souls.

God longs to satisfy our deepest desires. Satan, the great deceiver, is right there, waiting to show us a seemingly simpler way—"No need to search the Scriptures, gather with believers, serve, or pour out your heart in prayer. Just eat this. Buy that. Say yes to that ungodly relationship. Pursue power and fame. It will feel great. And it's easy."

What calls to you in moments of weakness? What do you use to quench that vague sense of emptiness? Buy more stuff you don't really need? Shop mindlessly for something, anything, to fill the void?

You can conquer the urge by pursuing your relationship with God. When those cravings hit, you can pause to consider the deeper meaning. By leaning on the One who always provides your needs, you can finally satisfy the longing and find contentment.

Angie

prayer

God, You know everything I've tried to find contentment.
Giving in to those cravings only led me farther away from You.
Father, I know that only You can fill the deepest longings in my heart.
Give me the strength to fight temptation and the wisdom to turn to
You instead.

roots of desire

Craving: a strong wanting of what promises enjoyment or pleasure.

As a self-avowed word nerd, I can't resist an opportunity to look up definitions. This one is particularly good for understanding the spiritual implications of our cravings. The "strong wanting" we feel is innate, a component of our soul. God designed us with deep desires.

Time and again, we misinterpret the craving. We're convinced that what we really need is a slice of chocolate cake. A remodeled kitchen. A long-term partner. A new dress. A promotion. Going back to the definition, these things "promise enjoyment or pleasure." But when we partake, they don't deliver. At least not long-term. Fooled again, we continue seeking, but not finding.

Use the categories below as cues to list specific cravings you've experienced:

- Food/drink
- Significance
- Connection/relationships
- Financial stability
- Peace/contentment

Briefly describe the circumstances surrounding each, and answer these questions:

- Where did the desire come from?
- Was it ever truly satisfied?
- Did you realize at the time that there was something else you were really craving? Or is that something you're realizing now?

Make a specific battle plan that includes Scripture, prayer, and/or anything else you determine to be appropriate for the situation. Note your battle plan here so it will be ready the next time you experience a craving for something you know won't really satisfy you.

Finally, pray over your plan. As you use it, record any observations and make adjustments as necessary. God longs for you to come to Him to meet your needs. He will be waiting with open arms!

reflection:

When you think about times when you've given in to unhealthy cravings, do you recall the Holy Spirit urging you not to give in? How can you be more attuned to the Spirit's nudge next time and rely on God to give you strength?

Reflections

day 10

How Much Is Enough?

"... give me neither poverty nor riches, but give me only my daily bread."
Proverbs 30:8 (NIV)

"How much is enough?" In the organizing world, it's such a tough question to answer. Somewhere between "not enough" and "too many" is overly vague. Like Goldilocks looking for a bed that's not too hard, not too soft, but just right, we're aiming for "just right." But how do we determine that quantity in a way that pleases God?

In our quest to define "enough" according to biblical standards, we're looking for our daily bread, that sweet spot that lies between poverty and riches described in Proverbs 30:8. Too little leaves us wanting; too much, and we're dishonoring God and dealing with clutter's consequences.

Wouldn't it be easier if someone just gave us the answer?

Instead of grappling with the issue, we'd love for someone to just give us a number already. A formula like "enough mugs in your kitchen=the number of people in the home x 2" would be welcomed. Maybe that's why the religious leaders were such fans of specifics. Give a tenth of your spices. Check. Done. No thinking involved.

Alas, it's never that simple. There's no magic formula. Even if there was, we can't guarantee that it will fit every situation or that we'll follow it perfectly. And even if we did follow the rules, it would be all for naught if our hearts weren't in the right place.

God longs for us to approach Him with our needs. He promises to supply them, but He doesn't promise to give us *everything* we want. When we remember that all we have comes from Him and make it our goal to use it all for His glory, we'll make better judgments in defining "enough."

The next time you're faced with a decluttering choice, instead of asking, "Do I have to get rid of this?" try asking, "Since I have enough of this item, and I'm not using this one, can I share it with someone else?" This simple change in wording not only reflects a change of heart that honors God, but also satisfies our quest for enough.

Angie

prayer

Lord, thank You for your promise to always meet my needs.
As I strive to understand how much is enough,
help me see my belongings for what they are—
gifts from You to be used for Your glory.
When I realize I have more than enough,
give me a willing heart to share the excess.

defining enough

Now it's time for a little practice in defining that ideal position somewhere between not enough and too many. We'll start by working through an example of a specific item.

Many people have an overabundance of T-shirts. Since they're frequent giveaways and souvenir purchases, we constantly add new ones. Some T-shirts have sentimental value, making it difficult to let go. If we're not careful, our collection can get out of control.

As I always tell my clients, everything you own belongs to you (okay, actually, it belongs to God, but you get the point), and it's completely your decision. However, our goal is to help you have a healthy relationship with your possessions and to eliminate clutter. An overabundance of T-shirts might be part of your clutter problem. (*Note: if you don't have a problem with T-shirts, try the same exercise using mugs or something else you tend to accumulate.)

How many T-shirts is enough?

1. How much space is being taken up by T-shirts? Is the space too crowded?

2. Estimate (or better yet, count) how many T-shirts you own. Record the number: _____

3. These questions will help you determine how few T-shirts would meet your needs.

   a. In an average week, how many T-shirts do you use?
   b. In an average week, how often do you do laundry?
   c. Given the above information, how few T-shirts would you need to own to have a clean one available every time you want to wear one? _____

4. What's the difference between the two numbers in questions #2 and #3? _____

5. Do you feel led to let some of your T-shirts go so someone else could use them? Pray for wisdom and a spirit of generosity.

Now, identify another category of belongings (or several) and complete the same exercise.

reflection:

What have you learned from completing this exercise? What will you do with this new understanding?

Reflections

day 11

What's That Stench?

"Then Moses said to them, "No one is to keep any of it (manna) until morning.' However, some of them paid no attention ... by morning it was full of maggots and began to smell."
Exodus 16:19-20 (NIV)

Every fall when the South Texas temperatures dip and provide us with a burst of slightly cooler air, there's nothing I love more than baking banana bread. It is an autumnal treat that lets me feel as if we actually have seasons here in the South.

Once made, I savor every bite of that moist cake. For breakfast, as a midday snack, as dessert after dinner. Needless to say, it doesn't last long in my house.

However, after baking my loaf this past year, I wasn't as committed to eating it as much as I normally do. So, it sat on the counter. For days. Each time I passed by it, I would tell myself to either eat it or throw it away. I did neither.

Finally, the craving hit. I couldn't wait to enjoy a slice of that sweet bread.

But when the first bite hit my tongue, I gagged. It wasn't just gross, it was rancid! No longer a delicacy to savor, I raced to the trash and spit it out as quickly as possible.

The incident reminded me of the Israelites who held on to the manna God had provided for them longer than they were supposed to. (They were only to keep it until morning.) The next day, it was full of maggots and stank. Not only did they have a terrible mess to clean up, but they also incurred Moses' anger.

The passage hit close to home after my unfortunate taste-testing.

How often do we hold on to things—banana bread, clothes that no longer serve us, utensils we don't need—longer than we should until they become an unwelcome odor in our spaces rather than a fragrant aroma? A burden rather than a joy?

Let's pay attention to what we have and when the time to say goodbye is drawing near for us to let go. When we do, not only will our homes be spaces that reflect what is truly important to us, but they will also be filled with a sweet perfume that will bless our families, our friends, and most importantly, our Lord.

Liana

prayer

Heavenly Father, teach us to recognize the moments
when we need to release what no longer serves us.
Just as the Israelites faced consequences for
holding onto manna past its time, guide us to let go gracefully.
May our lives be a fragrant offering, free from burdens,
and filled with the sweet perfume of joy.

expired!

Most of our food comes with an expiration date, an easy indicator of when we need to discard it. But what about everything else? How do we know when something—such as toiletries or other essentials—have passed their prime?

Since we don't want to wait until a stench permeates our home, let's go on the offensive and do a quick expiration check in and around our spaces:

kitchen

Before heading out to the grocery store, take a few minutes to go through your refrigerator, freezer, and pantry and check for items that might be expired or close to being expired. If the use-by date has passed, throw it away; if it hasn't, and you know you won't be using the food item, consider donating it to your local food pantry.

bathroom

Check all your lotions and shampoos for their expiration date (usually stamped on the bottom of the bottle), as well as your makeup. Most cosmetics are good for up to a year, but mascara and eyeliner have a short lifespan of about three months. For more specific expiration guidelines, google "Makeup/Toiletry Expiration Guidelines" for help.

Medicines, both prescribed and over-the-counter, should not be kept longer than the stated expiration dates. Certain medications are at risk of bacterial growth, leading to more serious illnesses if taken once their time has lapsed. Go through your medicine cabinet and gather any medicines that are no longer being used or have exceeded their timeframe and properly dispose of them at your local pharmacy or police station.

everything else

While there is no set expiration date on items such as clothing or toys, a good standard of practice is the one-year rule—if it hasn't been used in a year, then let it go!

reflection:

What have you been holding onto past its expiration date? How has it become a stench in your life and home?

Reflections

day 12

A Time to Let Go

*"... a time to scatter stones and a time to gather them, a time to embrace
and a time to refrain, a time to search and a time to give up, a time to
keep and a time to throw away ..."*
Ecclesiastes 3:5-6 (NIV)

It was time.

The soles of my favorite silver sandals were worn paper-thin. Ten years of constant use had taken its toll. Every time I slipped those shoes on for an outing, I knew I would slide them off in pain.

It was time I let go.

But I couldn't. I was certain I would never find another pair of sandals with such unique style and flair. They were my go-to shoes, my favorites, the ones I couldn't travel without. How could I possibly get rid of them?

Yet, my season for these beautiful sandals had surpassed the time they were intended. They did the job they were supposed to do—and then some. It was only fitting that I say goodbye to them so I could make space for a new pair.

It was time I let go for good.

While you may not have trouble parting with a certain pair of shoes, you likely have other items in your home that you are endeared to—your old, comfy jeans; the worn-out stuffed animal that's missing an eye; the trophies you won in high school that remind you of your glory days.

There was a proper season for those things, but now it may be time to let them go once and for all. It's never easy, but it's usually necessary. When we do, we are no longer bound by things that tie us down, bring us stress, or cause us pain. Instead, we can live with peace and freedom.

But we'll never see those results if we continue to cling to the things that no longer serve us. It's only when we let go that we can receive what's waiting for us in the next season of life.

Liana

prayer

Father, give me the strength I need to remove the unnecessary
so the essential has first place in my life.
Help me make room for that which serves me well and brings glory
to You.
Loosen my grip on what I need to let go of so my hands
will be free to receive all You have for me.

when is it time to let go?

How do you know when it's time to let go of a pair of shoes, a piece of clothing, an unused kitchen appliance, or anything else in your house? Is it a feeling you get, or are there visual indications that an item you own is no longer serving you?

While there's no definitive guide to dictate when or what to remove from your home, here are a few signs it might be time to part ways with your physical stuff:

- Dust collecting on the item
- Tears/rips, broken or missing parts, rendering it useless
- It's been crammed in the back of your drawer or closet, and you haven't missed it
- It no longer works properly and makes it hard to use
- You have no idea what it is or how to use it
- You've had it for a while, and it's still in its original packaging, untouched, or has the price tag attached
- Its "best by" date has passed

As you work through different rooms or spaces in your house, keep this list handy to help you determine whether or not to hold onto an item. In most cases, you'll find you can probably discard or donate the item without any regrets. Whatever it was had its season in your life. Now, it's time to let it go.

reflection:

Which of these signs did you notice most often as you worked through your stuff? What does that indicate to you?

Reflections

day 13

Glory Days

"Forget the former things; do not dwell on the past. See, I am doing a new thing!
Now it springs up; do you not perceive it?"
Isaiah 43:18-19 (NIV)

Best Defensive Player. All Conference. Academic All-American. Athlete of the Year. Most Valuable Player.

My trophies, plaques, and ribbons that adorned my childhood bedroom represented thousands of hours of "sweat equity" earned on volleyball courts, basketball courts, tracks, and softball fields. Every day after school, my teammates and I perfected our skills. I recall riding on the bus to games, my stomach full of butterflies. By game time, I was on edge but ready to give 100 percent. Bring. It. On.

For many years, these mementos were stored in the attic, reminders of my past life. They sparked a flood of memories: last-second shots at the buzzer, leaning in at the finish line, diving to get a hand on the volleyball to keep it in play. These relics of the past represented a life stage that defined me for so long.

Over the years as I transitioned from college student to wife to mother, I occasionally rediscovered the trophies. But now they brought sadness. When I was winning trophies, I felt like somebody special. As a full-time mother and community volunteer, I sometimes felt like a nobody.

I finally decided to stop looking back wistfully at my glory days. As wonderful as those memories were, I needed to focus on making new ones. My competitive nature and drive could still serve me well, even though my life was completely different. It was time to trust that God had great plans for my future. In order to be open to those plans, I needed to make room in my home, but more importantly, I needed to make room in my heart.

What are you holding onto? Are mementos from your glory days cluttering up your home and your heart? God has big plans for your future, but you've got to release your hold on the past first. It's time to embrace the new things God has in store for you.

Bring. It. On.

Angie

prayer

Father, you are so good. You loved me
and had a plan for me
even before You created me.
I want my identity to be wrapped up in
being Your child.
Thank You for giving me a purpose that matters so much more than
winning a trophy.
I'll go where You send me,
trusting that You know best.

embracing the now

Of all the belongings a person owns, mementos are probably the most difficult to declutter. These items tug on our emotions, and we may feel like getting rid of them devalues the memories and people involved.

While there's nothing wrong with holding onto treasures from the past, we can't keep every sentimental item. I believe in the mantra, "If everything is special, nothing is special." In a huge collection of keepsakes, individual items lose value. Our space is limited, and the more we keep from the past, the less space we have for the present and future.

action steps:

Think about the sentimental items you've saved from your life, any handed down from family members, and any you are saving for family members. If necessary, take a few minutes to look in the spaces where these items are stored. Answer the following questions:

1. How much space is being used for storing your mementos? Could these spaces be better used in another way?
2. If the mementos are stored in containers, how well do you know the contents? When was the last time you looked at

them? Could some or all of them be useful for someone else?

3. How do you feel about letting some or all of them go?
4. Do you have some additional space for special items you might decide to keep in the future?
5. Spend some time in prayer, asking God to show you any changes that you might need to make to embrace where you are now and His future plans for you.
6. Share what you learned from these action steps with someone who can encourage you and hold you accountable.

reflection:

With whom could you share what you learned while taking these action steps? Choose someone who can encourage you and hold you accountable for completing the work.

Reflections

day 14

You Can't Take It with You

"For we brought nothing into the world, and we can take nothing out of it."
1 Timothy 6:7 (NIV)

Dust particles floated through the air and tickled my nose as I pushed open the heavy curtains covering my hotel window. Basking in the warm sunlight that permeated the small space, I scanned the horizon in search of scenic beauty. Instead, my eyes fell on a shipping warehouse, jostling with activity, and a gray, forlorn cemetery that wasn't.

Mesmerized by the tombstones, which seemed to rise and fall along the brown grass like the rhythmic waves on a heart monitor, I instinctively reflected on the brevity of life and the uncertainty of tomorrow.

My somber thoughts, however, were interrupted by the noisy trucks below. Shifting my gaze, I watched the workers load box after box of material wares into the rigs. As I did, a stark reality struck me. There were no U-Hauls or storage units next to the final resting places of the deceased.

When they'd drawn their last breaths, they'd left everything behind. Childhood memorabilia faded by time, plates received as wedding gifts, the (no longer stylish) outfit worn on that one special occasion. Not a single person buried in that graveyard was able to hold onto their beloved keepsakes.

Yet, how many of us live as if we can?

All too often, we cling to the worldly goods we've accumulated over the years—storing them up and refusing to let them go—as if a heavenly moving container with them inside will follow us once we're gone.

But a cemetery is proof that isn't the case.

When your time on earth is up, all your possessions, whether few or many, will be distributed to family and friends, donated to strangers, or relegated to the trash. Usually in a large truck.

While there's still breath in your lungs, determine how you can have a healthier relationship with your stuff and focus on leaving behind what's truly important. A legacy of love, faith, and service.

Liana

prayer

Father, thank You for reminding me not only of how short this life is
but that in the end, the things of this world don't matter as much as I
thought.
Help me to understand that they are only temporary things
for me to enjoy as I travel toward my eternal home with You.

swedish death cleaning

Have you ever heard of the term *döstädning*? It's a popular Swedish tradition combining the words "do" (which means death) and "standing" (which means cleaning). The purpose behind the Swedish Death Cleaning craze is to get rid of all the stuff you've accumulated (and that you no longer need) so no one has to do it for you after you pass.

Yet, decluttering isn't easy when you have a lifetime worth of stuff to go through! To help you with the process, here are a few questions to ask yourself as you consider each item:

- Do I love it or just like it?
- When was the last time I used it? (Rule of thumb: If it hasn't been used in a year, let it go.)
- Does it still work?
- Do I have another one just like it or one that works better?
- If it's clothing, is it the right size, still in style, flattering, comfortable, and easy to wear?
- Could you rent it, borrow it, or find it (or the information about it) somewhere else?
- Could you capture it in another form? (i.e., a picture or a small piece to remember it)

- If you got rid of it, would you still have the emotion, the memory, or the experience that went with it?
- Do you have bad feelings associated with it?
- Is it too difficult or complicated to use, put together, or store?
- Who are you really keeping this for—you or someone else?
- What's the worst thing that could happen if you let it go?

Participating in the Swedish Death Cleaning ritual isn't suggesting you're dying any time soon. It simply allows you to enjoy what matters most to you now and doesn't burden your loved ones with the task later. It's truly one of the best gifts you can leave.

You might also want to consider gifting your loved ones some of your items that no longer serve you while you're still alive. Not only will you get to see them enjoy your gift, but you'll also be creating precious memories for them as well.

reflection:

Why are we so loath to declutter? How could it make a difference for you and your loved ones, both now and later?

Reflections

day 15

Hang Up Your Cape

"Moses' father-in-law replied, "What you are doing is not good ...
The work is too heavy for you; you cannot handle it alone."
Exodus 18:17-18 (NIV)

"Can I help you with that?" my co-worker asked after hearing me release another groan of frustration in the direction of my computer. My third in twenty minutes.

"No, I've got it, thanks," I mumbled, scrunching my forehead at the numbers and symbols on the spreadsheet before me.

"Okay." She turned her attention back to her work, probably shaking her head at my clear unwillingness to admit I was struggling.

She wasn't wrong. I had no clue how to make sense of the information on my screen, but I refused to accept her help.

That's because I always "think" I should be able to handle or complete whatever I'm facing by myself. It's usually easier that way, plus I don't want to bother or inconvenience anyone with my problems.

However, I'm not superwoman. I don't wear a cape, and I don't possess special powers. When I pretend that I do, I'm acting from a place of pride.

According to Scripture, God didn't create us to operate on our own. And He didn't give us the talents to do so either. Rather, He gave each of us gifts so when one of us is weak in an area, someone else who excels there can walk alongside us and carry the load.

When we insist on flying solo, we not only wear ourselves out trying to do it all, but we also rob others of an opportunity to shine by showcasing their skills, and we allow the sin of pride to dwell in our hearts.

Is there something you're facing today—a work project or a household task—you need help with? Why not hang up your cape and look around to see who might be willing or capable to assist you? Then consider taking the bold step to ask him or her for help. When you do, you'll not only be a blessing, but be blessed as well.

Liana

prayer

Lord, may I not be a superhero,
trying to do it all myself.
Help me to remember that You have
given each of us
gifts to use for Your glory and others' benefit.
Open my eyes to those moments when
I can use my talents
and when I need to step aside and
let others shine.

only what you can do

Andy Stanley, pastor of North Point Ministries in Georgia, once said, "Only do what only you can do."

For those of us who find it hard to ask for assistance, accept help, or delegate tasks to others, that's a profound statement.

But it's true. There are things that *only we can do*. For everything else, we need to consider letting others do those tasks or accept others' efforts to help us. We simply can't do it all ourselves, so let's stop trying.

Think about all the tasks on your to-do list for today or the upcoming week. Then, file each one under one of the following:

things only i can do

_____
_____
_____

things others can do

_____

_____

_____

Using the list as your guide, focus on doing what only you can do, then seek out others who could handle the rest, whether by asking or delegating. While it may seem hard to do at first, you'll be surprised at others' willingness and excitement to help you. Not only that, but in doing so, you'll find more joy and peace in your day and schedule too.

reflection:

What discoveries did you make by listing out what only you can do and what tasks you can delegate to others? How has that changed your perspective on being a superhero?

Reflections

day 16
Untangled

"... let us throw off everything that hinders and the sin that so easily entangles ..."
Hebrews 12:1 (NIV)

The dead tree stood in our backyard for months. We kept hoping it would spring back to life one day and present us with an array of colorful blooms and sweet fragrances during the summer months, but it never did. So, when a storm came through and easily knocked off several of its limbs, we had no choice but to chop it down.

While I was sad to see it go, I couldn't help but notice the effect its dismantling had on the trees that had been intertwined with it. As each defunct limb was removed, the branches of other nearby trees sprang to life. They were no longer weighed down by the dead offshoots and slowly returned to their upright positions. It was as if they were given a new chance at life. Beautifully, they reached up toward the sky and danced in the wind like they were supposed to.

I've learned the hard way that if we aren't careful, we, too, can become like those nearby trees whose branches are held down by others.

In the past, I've allowed myself to become encumbered by so many commitments on my schedule that I was anxious and exhausted by it all. But rather than slow down, I just kept adding more responsibilities to my plate.

Then, I was diagnosed with a health issue that forced me to prune some unnecessary tasks off my to-do list. As I did, I slowly came back to life. No longer weighed down by so much activity, I had space to breathe and move the way I was supposed to. Just like those newly released tree limbs.

What if we unchained ourselves from the obligations and responsibilities that we add to our calendars because "we should," "we have to," or because "no one else will do it"? What if we removed the barren activities (those that don't bring us joy or aren't fruitful) from our lives and made room for the life-giving tasks that bless us and others?

Who could we be and what could we accomplish? We'll only find out once we're willing to become untangled.

Liana

prayer

Lord, untangle me from all the activities
that keep me from being who You've
called me to be.
Give me the courage to prune them from
my life and schedule so I can make room for the
tasks that will be not only a blessing to me, but to others as well.

decluttering your schedule

They say you can tell a person's priorities by their checkbooks and their calendars. Since we don't want to peek into your finances, we'll tackle your calendar instead.

While it wouldn't be realistic to remove all activity from your life, let's simply take a look at the next few days of tasks/responsibilities/commitments and see if we might be able to untangle them a bit so you are free to be who and what you were created for.

1. Go through each activity you have listed on your calendar or schedule for the next 3 days and jot them down on the reflections page.
2. Next to each one, write whether it is something that is non-negotiable (like picking up your kids from school or shopping for groceries), a should do, a must do because no one else will, or a non-essential/non-fruitful.
3. Study your list and pray about which of those you listed as a should do, a must do because no one else will, or a non-essential/non-fruitful task that can be pruned from your schedule (hopefully, most of them!).
4. If possible, go ahead and remove the non-essentials from your schedule (and make arrangements for someone else to

handle them). If you're having trouble delegating, refer to Day 15—Hang Up Your Cape.

5. With your calendar untangled (somewhat), write down how it feels to be "free" from those obligations and what it might mean for you moving forward.

6. Then, spend time in prayer seeking God's guidance and wisdom now that you're no longer weighed down.

7. Repeat this activity until you're satisfied with the way your calendar/schedule looks and feels.

reflection:

What activities were keeping you weighed down? How hard was it to prune them from your calendar? How can you keep from becoming tangled again?

Reflections

day 17

Don't Break the Chain

*"Three times a day he (Daniel) got down on his knees and prayed,
Giving thanks to his God, just as he had done before."*
Daniel 6:10 (NIV)

When I see successful people, I want to know what they did to get to that position. Sure, a few people may find overnight success, but the majority of people who got to the top didn't just arrive there. They climbed.

So, I studied the habits and routines of these success stories. While there are many interesting tales of what people did to become someone others emulated, the one who caught my attention the most was Jerry Seinfeld.

When Jerry was first starting as a comedian, he would write one joke a day. He had a one-year wall calendar hanging in his office, and every day after writing his lone funny quip, he would cross out that day with a large, red *X*. Ultimately, his goal was to not break the chain —no empty spots allowed.

In doing so, he became one of the most famous comedians of our time. All because he developed a routine and stuck with it.

But he is one of the rare few.

For most people, routines carry a negative connotation. Many choose not to add daily practices into their lives, complaining they are stifling, boring, and uncreative. In actuality, routines offer more freedom by taking the guesswork out of what needs to be done. They provide more focus, leading to higher productivity and, overall, creating less stress.

Even in biblical times, routines were important. Consider Daniel's habit of prayer, Jesus' routine of going away to be alone with his Father, and Paul's consistent practice of going to the synagogue when he arrived in a new city. Each of them understood the need and the power of implementing routines into their daily lives. If they exemplified that discipline, shouldn't we?

From heroes of the faith to modern-day celebrities, we can't underestimate the benefits of routines. When added to our schedules, they are a formidable tool that can allow us to get more done. But only if we're careful and don't break the chain.

Liana

prayer

Father, thank You for the examples
You've set before me.
Help me to learn from them and
give me the strength
to follow in their footsteps.
Remove any negative thing from my mind
so that I might be able to develop the habits and
discipline I need to grow both spiritually and
in my efforts to get organized.

wash. rinse. repeat.

James Clear, the author of *Atomic Habits*, states in his book, "Too often we convince ourselves that massive results require massive action." That's especially true when we want to develop routines. But what if we started small, with one tiny action that, when multiplied over time, led to massive results?

Most routines generally fail because people try to add too many actions at once or they have unrealistic expectations of what they want to accomplish. In this Unclutter It, we're going to keep it simple and focus on one small routine. While it may seem insignificant in size or effort, repeatedly practicing this tiny habit can develop your organizing muscles so you can slowly but surely bring order to your life.

Choose one of the routines below (or feel free to pick your own) and see how many days you can go without breaking the chain. After time, it will become automatic, just like shampooing your hair: Wash. Rinse. Repeat.

routine options:

- Spend 5 minutes putting things where they belong at the end of each day.

- Remove 5 items you no longer need, use, or want from your house each day (have a box handy to dispose of items, then donate when the box is full).
- Spend 5 minutes each day decluttering a pile (paper, clothes, toys) in your house.
- Make your bed each day.
- Deal with things (bills, papers, items) immediately rather than waiting for later.

You can do this! Even small habits can guide your life to a different destination. What are you waiting for? Start today and discover all the places you'll go!

reflection:

How might committing to a small routine impact your daily life? What do you think could be the long-term effects on your overall well-being and organization?

Reflections

day 18

On the Daily

"Lazy hands make for poverty, but diligent hands bring wealth."
Proverbs 10:4 (NIV)

I'm not a fan of visiting the dentist. While I dislike the sound of the hygienist's tools scraping tartar off my teeth, I love rolling my tongue across my freshly polished pearly whites afterward.

Early in our marriage, my husband and I realized we hadn't scheduled a dentist appointment in a while and hadn't been flossing regularly. That next cleaning was particularly brutal, but that was the price we paid for neglecting our oral hygiene. Brushing and flossing are not habits that can be relegated to a weekly, monthly, or (heaven forbid) yearly basis. They must be done daily to be effective.

The same principle applies to just about any routine. I have noticed that a large percentage of my clients' clutter is related to inconsistent implementation of household routines. A kitchen sink piled high with dirty dishes, while clean ones remain on the counter, untouched. Laundry in baskets—on beds or on the floor. Grocery bags filled with items that weren't put away. Suitcases never fully unpacked after a trip.

Like a constant reminder of looming tasks, visual clutter contributes to depression and a feeling of being overwhelmed. All of these situations can be remedied with consistent routines.

While there are no direct biblical mandates like, "Thou shalt do laundry daily," or "The fool leaves his tote bag filled," the Bible does point to the rewards of diligence and hard work. In Proverbs alone, we find these rewards: profit, wealth, abundance, and the power to rule.

The challenge in establishing and maintaining daily routines is in both the planning and the doing. We don't magically have openings in our schedule for tasks like dishes, laundry, and daily pickup. Talking about consistent routines is great, but it's the hard work of our diligent hands that brings the reward. It requires a concerted effort to both manage the time for routines and to accomplish them.

But there's no doubt it's worth the effort. Clean teeth and clear counters are wonderful things.

Angie

prayer

Lord, Your Word clearly teaches that diligence and hard work reap
rewards.
Help me to honor You with my daily actions.
When I'm tempted to slack off or to be lazy,
remind me of Scriptures that point to the value of consistent labor
so I can practice regular habits to take care of myself, my home, and
my family.

Now, Unclutter it!

give me five!

Consistent implementation of household routines does wonders for clutter prevention. A five-minute daily pickup is one of the single best practices for keeping an orderly home. It's quick and easy, and it lends itself to the whole family's participation.

Just like with any habit, it may take a little while for it to become instinctive. But over time, you'll see tremendous results.

The best time of the day for a five-minute pickup is whatever time you're most likely to fit it in. Choose what works best for you and your schedule, then get going!

1. Include everyone in the home. If you have children, try making it fun, using a timer, music, or any other technique to make it seem less like work and more like play. We're all more likely to do something if it's enjoyable, right?
2. Choose your words carefully. We can usually endure an unpleasant task for five minutes, but if we announce— "Okay, everyone! We're going to tidy up the whole house. Ready?"—you might be met by groans and eye rolls. Instead, try—"Give me five!"—which sounds a lot more manageable. Then, set a timer and get to work.

3. There will be several categories of items you'll encounter in the five-minute pickup:

- Trash is an easy and frequent category, so have everyone take a small plastic bag along with them to save the steps it takes to throw away each item.
- If you recycle, you may need a different bag for that.
- Items that have an established "home" or place they belong can be quickly taken there.
- "Homeless" belongings with no clear location are the most difficult. If there are several of them, gather them into a container to deal with later. Try not to get bogged down with anything for long. Focus on making as much progress as you can in five minutes.

When the timer goes off, celebrate your accomplishment!

reflection:

When would be the best time during your day for a five-minute pickup? How can implementing this practice on a regular basis make a difference?

Reflections

day 19

Peace in the Busy Season

"Be very careful, then, how you live—not as unwise but as wise, making the most of every opportunity, because the days are evil."
Ephesians 5:15-16 (NIV)

We've all had them—seasons when we're just trying to survive.

We long to toss the to-do list out the window and clear the calendar completely. Optional events are skipped, and we're lucky to just get everyone in the household clothed, fed, and transported to their activities.

During chaotic times, it's easy to feel overwhelmed and wonder how we'll ever conquer our to-do list. The simple answer is we can't. And we don't necessarily need to. In fact, it's good for our physical, mental, and spiritual health to take a few things off our plates when life is exceptionally busy.

While some tasks can't be put aside, others are great candidates for temporary back-burner status. At some point, we have to make the tough decision to prioritize tasks that are indispensable to our well-being while opting out of the optional.

It's a delicate dance.

The truth is we can't run on empty. Just as it would be ludicrous to refrain from eating or sleeping for no reason, we can't skip feeding our souls, either. In the midst of a frantic frenzy, you may feel you don't have time to spend in God's Word or prayer, but we need spiritual nourishment *every day*, especially in a season of high demand.

In addition to feeding our bodies and souls, we're obligated to fulfill our commitments. While your boss might be willing to grant your request for a day off on your anniversary, I'm not sure a week off to catch up on gift-wrapping would be approved.

Just as Jesus perfectly prioritized time with His Father, even in the busiest of times, we need to seek God's guidance on prioritizing the essentials and minimizing the nonessentials.

And when the stress of those tasks we've pushed to the back burner weighs on our minds, He can help us keep it all in perspective. By aligning our mindset with the eternal perspective of God's Word, we can be at peace in the busiest of seasons.

Angie

prayer

Lord, You know the pattern of my days
and how difficult it is for me when my schedule is more full than
usual.
When I'm in a busy season of life, teach me to model Jesus
by making time with You my priority.
Give me peace about the tasks that must remain undone for a season.

naming the essentials

The best time to prepare for a busy season is *before* it happens, not in the midst of the quandary. It's time to make an action plan so that the next time you have extra demands on your time, you'll be ready!

prepare your list:

- Start by making a list of your regular activities. Focus more on jotting them all down quickly and less on organizing them or making the list look neat and tidy. Yes, you read that correctly; it doesn't have to be organized (yet).
- Add to your list by consulting your paper or digital schedule. You only need to write down the names of the activities; don't worry about details.
- Add anything that isn't currently a regular activity but that you intend to add. Hint—if you don't have a regular habit of prayer and Bible study, here's your opportunity to include it.

name the essentials:

- It's time to name the essentials. If you have a tendency to get easily overwhelmed, you may already be feeling that way. Don't worry; we're going to unclutter it!

- Consider every item individually. Put a star beside and circle the absolutes, activities that should be prioritized, even when demands are high. These are your front-burner items—the ones you will always do, no matter what.
- The rest of the list is your back-burner activities. When things heat up, give yourself permission to let these go for a while.

pray:

- Spend some time with God reflecting on this list. Thank God for the rich life He's given you that's full of opportunities. Ask Him to show you anything that isn't labeled as it should be, anything that is missing, or anything that should be omitted altogether. Pray for peace with the decisions you've made and for peace when it's time to put this list to the test.

reflection:

Are there any upcoming seasons of life when you might need to put this exercise into practice? After you've determined your essentials, how can you make sure the back-burner activities stay on the back burner the next time your schedule is overloaded?

Reflections

day 20

Unplugged

"Set your minds on things above, not on earthly things."
Colossians 3:2 (NIV)

I have a love/hate relationship with my phone.

As a lover of technology, I rely on it for a myriad of reasons: reminders, contact information, email, and much more. Even my recipes are digital. And I'd be literally lost without GPS. Our phones are powerful tools, but if we don't exercise restraint, they can easily clutter our minds and cause us not to pay attention to what's most important.

A few years ago, I finally admitted I was addicted to my phone. Like most addictions, there were serious consequences. The price I paid was a considerable one. Hours of scrolling on my phone translated into neglect of my husband, children, and extended family. Intentionally or not, when glued to my phone, I was communicating to my loved ones that my phone was more important than them.

How I wish I could turn back the clock and erase the damage.

Ultimately, it was my relationship with God that suffered most. My mind was set squarely on earthly things. My social media feeds, the latest news, and my to-do list were at the forefront of my mind, while thoughts of things above were nonexistent.

Praise God I finally "came to my senses" and got serious about turning back to God and to my family. Repentance required drastic steps. My phone detox included no charging by the bedside, no phone use during meals, and turning off loads of notifications, among other things. Breaking that dependence was difficult, and it's an ongoing process. I still reach for my phone far too often, and I continue to look for new ways to reduce my screen time.

I'm not alone in this battle. Phone addiction is widespread, spanning all ages, genders, and demographics. If you can relate to this struggle, I want to reassure you that change is not only possible, but with God's power, it is assured!

Is it time for you to face the truth that you're more plugged in than is healthy? Are you ready to take the necessary steps to unplug? I guarantee that you'll strengthen your most important relationships. They're the ones that really matter.

Angie

prayer

Father, I'm thankful for my phone and
all the ways it makes my life easier.
But I recognize that my dependence on it is causing me
to neglect my loved ones and to neglect my relationship with You.
With Your strength, I know I can put it in its proper place in my life.

how much time is it, really?

As you read the "Unplugged" devotional, your thoughts probably resembled one of these:

1. I know exactly what she's talking about. I've got a problem with that too!
2. I don't have a problem with too much phone time, but (insert name here) sure does!

No matter which of the above describes your thoughts, you still need this exercise. Even if you don't think you have a problem, you may be surprised—even shocked—to find out how much time you're spending on your phone. Facing the truth was crucial for identifying and fighting my phone addiction. By the way, this exercise applies to time on any digital device, not just phones, so don't neglect to consider time on your tablet, laptop, or digital watch as well.

So, how much time are you actually spending on your phone? Our smartphones are smart enough to give us the answers, if we let them. You can find your average screen time per day, which apps you've used and for how long, how many times per day you pick up your phone, and much more. I encourage you to search for specific up-to-date instructions to find out these numbers on your particular smartphone. You may find it interesting to guess these numbers beforehand.

What you do with the information is your decision. But I implore you to learn from my mistakes. Whether the numbers are higher or lower than average, you may still have a problem.

If you really want to know if this is a problem, ask your loved ones. Ask questions like, "Does my phone damage our time together?"; "Do I seem distracted by my phone?"; or "I worry I use my phone too much. Do you agree?" Then be prepared to hear the honest answers.

There is no greater gift you can give a person than your full attention. Decreasing your phone use is an excellent way to give your full attention, which communicates your love.

reflection:

How do you feel about finding out how much time you spend on your electronic devices? Who will you talk to (and when) about your phone use and its effects?

Reflections

day 21

The Seasonality of Relationships

"God has said, 'I will never fail you. I will never abandon you.'"
Hebrews 13:5b (NLT)

Giving and receiving Christmas cards is one of my favorite holiday traditions. I enjoy photos and updates from family and friends we don't connect with on a regular basis as well as from those we do. As we prepare to send our family year in review and family picture, we look over the names of people in our Christmas card contacts. Often we've made new friends during the year, so the list grows.

But when the list of card recipients becomes too long, unfortunately we must do some decluttering.

If we just kept adding people but never subtracted, eventually we'd be sending more cards than we'd like, making the task time-consuming and expensive. Removing people from the list seems harsh, but if we don't have much of a connection anymore, it's a logical choice.

I loathe these decisions, sometimes agonizing over them. Not necessarily because of the card itself, but because it represents a change in the relationship. The simple truth is, we can't ignore that friends come and go. It's unrealistic to think we could maintain close relationships with everyone we've been close to over the years. Friendships have a certain seasonality about them. Only a select few stand the test of time.

The grief over a changed relationship can be troublesome when the connection ends unpleasantly. Disagreements can cause us to cut ties suddenly. The most painful transition is when a friendship simply fizzles out, especially when there has been no inciting event. One party may have simply disappeared, leaving the other feeling abandoned, confused, and hurt.

Every human is fallible, every relationship tenuous. Our heavenly Father is the only One on Whom we can depend. God knows every hurt you've endured, every tear you've cried. And when we pour out our sorrows to Him, He comforts us with a love beyond comprehension. Oh, that we would learn to trust in Him only, to let every life situation draw us ever closer into His loving arms.

He never fails us.

Angie

prayer

Holy Father, thank You for the gift of friendship. You have blessed me
with so many friends who have made my life richer.
Some of these friendships have ended before I felt ready, and I miss
them.
I'm grateful that You know each person and each situation, that You
can help me address the emotions, and that Your love never fails.

relationship check-up

While it's true that our relationship with God is our most important one by far, that doesn't mean earthly relationships aren't valuable. Connections with family and friends are some of God's greatest gifts. Our Father knows that having like-minded companions with whom to go through both victories and trials is a key ingredient for happiness.

And yet we know that friendships often fail to go the distance. Whatever the reason the relationship changes, we are often left mourning the demise of a close friendship. How do we manage the sorrow in a healthy way? We take it to the only One who can heal us.

- Begin by jotting down the names of people whose presence in your life is a joy and by thanking God for them. Pray also for the wisdom and courage to address conflict with these individuals quickly and biblically.
- Next, write the names of past relationships. Ask God to reveal any situation that still needs to be resolved. Ask for His healing touch on your heart and to be drawn closer to Him. Pray for these friends to be blessed with God's peace. Thank God for His unconditional love and acceptance.

reflection:

How has God used past friendships that are no longer active to bless you during a specific season of life? How have you done the same for others?

Reflections

day 22

A Godly Perspective on Your
To-Do List

*"Since we are living by the Spirit, let us follow the Spirit's
leading in every part of our lives."*
Galatians 5:25 (NLT)

My husband and I live in a small loft and both work from home. On weekdays, we have breakfast and lunch together, but we work in separate rooms.

After work, we always ask each other, "How was your day?" This is slightly comical since we've been together much of the day. What we really mean is, "How was work?"

Following is a typical weekday afternoon conversation at the Hyche home:

Me: "How was your day?"

Hubby: "Great! Got a lot done. Not many meetings. How was your day?"

Me: "Just okay. Not much accomplished."

Our answer always has two parts: an adjective and an elaboration based on productivity.

There's nothing wrong with measuring success by work accomplished, but I'd prefer to evaluate my day on a spiritual level. My to-do list and I have a complicated relationship—it's both my best friend and worst enemy. A prioritized to-do list keeps me focused. But as a perfectionist, I sometimes feel enslaved to that blasted list.

It's well past time to dethrone it.

I need a new tool for building my list and a new measuring stick. How did Jesus decide what to do? How did He rate himself? Jesus' sole focus on earth was to accomplish God's will, to do exactly what God wanted. Period.

How can we follow Jesus' example and serve God through our work? We can start by aligning ourselves with God's will. And we can listen for the guidance of the Holy Spirit to direct our day.

Perhaps soon, our evening conversations can be different.

Hubby: "How was your day?"

Me: "Wonderful! I prayed over my to-do list, and based on the Spirit's lead, I ended up working on something else entirely. I didn't mark much off the list, but I'm confident I did what God wanted me to do today."

I love the sound of that, don't you? I think Jesus would too.

Angie

prayer

I long to do Your work, God,
not just to check off tasks on my list.
I long to submit to Your Spirit when He prompts me to
follow a different plan than the one I've made.
Thank You for sending Jesus to model a life
of serving You perfectly.

Now, Unclutter it!

a closer inspection

During this Unclutter It, you'll examine your to-do list with a spiritual magnifying glass and make changes if needed.

The goal is to align your daily actions at home and work with God's will for your life, adjusting according to the Spirit's lead.

1. Review your current to-do list(s). You may have more than one; for example, I keep a to-do list for home and one for work.
2. Now make a list of your top priorities. If you're like me, you might have automatic answers that reflect what your priorities *should be*, not necessarily what they are right now. And that's okay—there may be further work to do later, but don't get carried away with that right now. Just make a short list of what is most important to you.
3. Compare the two lists. Does your to-do list line up with what you've identified as your primary concerns? This comparison isn't always straightforward. Often the tasks on our list represent a more overarching goal.
4. Pray over both of your lists. Ask the Father to give you a spiritual perspective so you can make adjustments. Write down anything you learn, and add, subtract, or rearrange as needed.

5. Repeating this exercise occasionally will help you stay focused on what God is calling you to do!

reflection:

Did your to-do list and your priorities align well? If not, how will you address this difference? How can you make sure they don't get misaligned in the future?

Reflections

day 23

Attention, Please

"Love the Lord your God with all your heart and with all your soul and with all your mind and with all your strength."
Mark 12:30 (NIV)

One Sunday morning I was gathered with believers, "raising a Hallelujah." Our voices joined in praise. During the sermon, while searching for a Scripture on my tablet, I jumped to email. It was a momentary diversion. A couple of quick taps on the screen. Suddenly, instead of praising God, I was fast-forwarded into the future, ticking off items on my to-do list. The sermon might have been perfect for my spiritual needs, but my distracted mind prevented me from hearing it.

While my home is a paragon of order, inside my mind, it's a completely different story. Often, actions and thoughts are completely mismatched, each going in opposing directions. It's called mental clutter, and it affects my ability to concentrate on the here and now.

It can also be dangerous.

While chopping vegetables, a lapse of attention could result in a nasty cut. Mindlessly scrolling social media may cause us to miss an appointment. During dinner with loved ones, we might be ruminating over our to-do list instead of listening.

Just as God wants us to love Him with all of our heart, soul, strength, *and mind*, our friends and family deserve our undivided attention too. The clutter of unnecessary thoughts draws us away from the present moment. By prioritizing the here and now above regrets about the past and worries about the future, we can give our full concentration to the situations and the people around us.

Consider your habits and your thought life. Is mental clutter an issue for you? What is God calling you to do so you can focus on the present? When you choose to be *all in* wherever you are and whatever you're doing, you'll be rewarded with a more intentional life and a closer relationship with your loved ones and your Heavenly Father. What a sweet reward!

Angie

prayer

Day 23

Father, we strive to love You with our hearts, souls, strength, and
minds.
But our minds are so prone to wander.
When our thoughts stray once again, help us catch them quickly
so we can honor those we love by giving them our full attention.
Grant us the ability to focus our minds on what is truly important.

meditation: a tool for focus

A few years ago, my Christian counselor encouraged me to try meditation as a tool for being more present in the moment, for combating distracting thoughts, and for coping with anxiety. As a person whose mind is constantly churning with thoughts, ideas, and worries and whose body is constantly on the move, sitting quietly without a task is a challenge for me. It took a while for meditation to go from a strange and awkward activity I avoided to a relaxing practice that I enjoyed. I can honestly report that a consistent habit of meditation has become a valuable tool.

Meditation sometimes gets a bad reputation. Many Christians shy away for fear that it's touchy-feely, New Age, or too closely related to Eastern religions, like Buddhism. Any tool can be used incorrectly, and God encourages us to closely examine everything against His Word. There are numerous Scriptures related to meditation and mindfulness. I recommend you do research if this is a concern for you.

If you've never tried meditation before, I encourage you to give it a try. Here are some tips to get you started if you're new to the practice.

- Since this is new for you, you'll probably benefit from a tool to help you get started. Not because it's difficult, but simply because it's new. I have enjoyed a free app called

Smiling Mind. There are plenty of other helpful resources you can find with an easy web search.

- Keep in mind that the overall purpose is learning to focus on the present moment. While meditating, you can choose to concentrate on breathing, a scan of your body, or the sounds around you. As distracting thoughts come into your mind, and they undoubtedly will, you'll learn how to deal with them.

Through regular practice, you'll get better at focusing on the present in your daily life. As a result, you'll be able to give your full attention to the task and people around you. Meditation can aid both your work life and your home life. Relationships are strengthened as you give full attention to the people around you. Most importantly, you can deepen your relationship with God. I can't think of a better outcome!

reflection:

When would be the best time during your day to practice meditation? What do you hope to gain from a meditation practice?

Reflections

day 24

Follow the Ants!

"Look to the ant ... it stores its provisions in summer and gathers its food at harvest."
Proverbs 6:6 (NIV)

There are two things you can be certain of when the calendar flips to June 1 in South Texas: mosquitoes and the start of hurricane season.

While there's not much we can do about the blood-sucking bugs, we can prepare for the potential of deadly storms. Batteries. Water. Flashlights. Food. It's the same routine every summer.

Yet, it's amazing the number of people who wait until the last minute to rush the grocery aisles—like troops storming the beaches of Normandy—to purchase the necessary supplies, only to find the shelves empty. No milk. No bread. Only cans of sardines and an assortment of herbal teas. Little do they realize, their lack of preparedness can have serious, even deadly, consequences.

That's why it's important that we look to the ants. Without being told, ants know the importance of preparing ahead of time, and they do it. They work hard and store up so when hard times fall, they don't have anything to worry about. Because of their diligence, ants have survived throughout the ages.

We would be wise to do the same.

Although we can never know when an emergency will arise, we can take necessary steps so the unexpected doesn't completely throw us off kilter—whether it be a financial setback, a natural disaster, a trip to the emergency room, or a late-night science project.

Not only does being prepared benefit us, but it also allows us to be available for others when they're in a bind, ready when God calls us to serve Him, armed to withstand the enemy and his attempts to sway us, and one day, set to welcome our Lord Jesus once more.

Ultimately, we can't control what happens to us, but we can control our effort and preparation (just be careful not to overprepare). In what areas of your life do you need to be better prepared today? What steps can you take now so when things go awry, you're found ready?

Liana

prayer

Lord, we don't know what tomorrow holds—only You do.
But we can be wise and do our best to be prepared.
Show me the areas of my life that I need
to pay more attention to and make the effort to be ready.
Thank You, Lord, that no matter what may come my way,
I know that You are in control, and I won't be shaken.

how ready are you?

For this Unclutter It! let's gauge your preparedness level by answering the following questions:

1. On a scale of 1-10, with 1 being poor and 10 being excellent, how well prepared are you for events and circumstances?
2. In what areas of your life do you feel well-prepared? What areas might you need to improve?
3. When was the last time you were prepared for an event/circumstance? How did being ready make you feel?
4. When was the last time you were unprepared for an event/circumstance? How did that lack of preparation cause you to feel?
5. How does being prepared bless others in your life? How does your unpreparedness affect them?

Now read the following passages and meditate on the importance of being prepared both practically and spiritually:

1. Matthew 25:1-13
2. Proverbs 28:19-20
3. 1 Peter 5:8
4. Mark 13:32-33

reflection:

What does it mean for you to be found ready? What steps do you need to take today to be prepared for what may come?

Reflections

day 25

Selfish Gifting

"Don't look out only for your own interests, but take an interest in others too."
Philippians 2:4 (NLT)

Every year as the holidays approach, I start feeling anxious about buying gifts. Some people are so difficult to buy for. Number one on that list—my husband. Since I know him better than anyone else, you'd think buying for him would be easy. The problem isn't getting ideas. The real dilemma? I don't want to give him what he really wants.

It's not that he asks for unhealthy things. He just requests the same boring and unoriginal gift every year. An Amazon gift card. And it doesn't even have to be wrapped, which is a bummer since I really enjoy wrapping!

When I consider why I find it so daunting to purchase something so simple, and something most people would happily purchase, I realize my reasons are selfish. In essence, the experience won't meet *my* expectations. I have a vision of surprising him with the perfect gift he didn't realize he wanted but was euphoric to get. It would be just like a Hallmark® movie.

While gifts are supposed to center on the recipient, the giver's preferences frequently factor into the equation, whether or not they should. Maybe a store is offering an amazing price on something, but that item isn't one the recipient would enjoy. Have you chosen a gift simply because it's quick and easy, even though you know it's not the best option? Ever been to a baby shower where the expectant mother had a gift registry, but 23 people ignored it and bought a cute newborn outfit because they couldn't resist? When we make choices like these when choosing gifts, we're in danger of spreading the clutter contagion to our loved ones.

I've made all of the above mistakes and more. Since then, I've chosen to put the gift recipient's interests first, not my own. If we could all strive to put the principle of placing others' interests above our own into practice, not only in gift-giving but also in our daily lives, we could rest assured we are imitating Jesus. And we'd give everyone exactly what they need, which would allow them to stay uncluttered. Perfect, right?

Angie

prayer

God, You've given us the perfect example, even in gift-giving!
You always put the needs of Your children above Your own.
I want to give just like You and Your Son.
When I'm tempted to selfishly put myself first
as I choose gifts for others, nudge me toward
Your perfect plan of selflessness.

a gifting plan

Most of us find pleasure in gift-giving. Expressing our love for another person by giving a gift is especially enjoyable when we're confident we've chosen something the recipient will like and be able to use. Try as we might to find the perfect selection, we sometimes fall short. The purpose of this Unclutter It is to examine and improve your gift-giving practices.

1. Describe your usual routine when choosing gifts. Does it include any of the following? Don't answer what you think you *should* do, but what you actually do. The goal is to examine and improve your practices.

- I look for or ask for a registry, wish list, or gift ideas, if possible.
- I ask the recipient, or close friends or family members of the recipient, for ideas.
- I choose an item I think the person might like that is currently on sale and popular.
- I spend time with the person to get to know them better so I can make better gift choices.
- I prioritize experiences (like tickets, memberships, etc.) and/or consumables (something that can be used up like food, toiletries, etc.) over physical gift items.

- I pick an item from a collection of pre-purchased gifts that I think the person might like.
- I search online for gift ideas based on what I know about the person.
- I choose something I already have but am not using that I think the person might like.
- I send a very general gift card so that they can use it for many different options.
- Other

2. What works about your current routine? What doesn't work?

3. How have your experiences with receiving unwanted gifts influenced your practices?

reflection:

After reading the devotional and working through this exercise, are there any changes you'd like to make in your gifting practices? How will you incorporate these changes?

Reflections

day 26

Do You Suffer from C.H.A.O.S.?

"Practice hospitality."
Romans 12:13b (NIV)

Ding-dong!

There's nothing that causes an icy chill to run down your spine more than the shrill ring of your doorbell.

You know what that means, right? Company's coming!

Halting in your tracks, you pray that whoever's on the other side of the door will quickly leave. Beads of perspiration fall to the floor as you survey the current condition of your house: dirty dishes piled up in the sink; toys scattered across the living room; paper stacks covering the kitchen counter; and worst of all, you haven't showered yet.

Ding-dong!

"Oh, please, Lord," you pray, "make them go away."

Time crawls until silence once again blankets your home. You exhale a huge breath of relief. Somehow, you've managed to avoid having people in your house.

Sound familiar? If so, then you probably suffer from C.H.A.O.S. —a nonmedical, completely made-up term for Can't Have Anyone Over Syndrome. A 'malady' that's growing exponentially these days, causing people to become more isolated and straining relationships.

The good news is, there's a cure. A simple mind shift, really, and one that can transform our outlook on inviting guests into our personal spaces: being hospitable and hosting people in our homes has nothing to do with us—it's about the ones we've invited in and meeting their needs.

Embracing this truth allows us to take our eyes off ourselves and understand that offering hospitality to others doesn't come from a fancy table that says, "Look at me and what I have." It comes from a loving heart that says, "What I have is yours, no matter how lovely or ugly it may look." It's an invitation into our hearts, homes, and lives with no thought of personal gain.

If you've been suffering from Can't Have Anyone Over Syndrome lately, know that there's hope. The antidote is to practice hospitality from God's perspective. When you do, you won't have to hide when your doorbell rings again.

Liana

prayer

Father, You've called us to be hospitable,
to love 'strangers.'
I know at times I haven't been willing
to open my doors to others
because of the condition of my home.
Forgive me.
Give me a heart and mind that takes the focus off myself and places it
on the needs of others. May I graciously and joyfully
welcome others into my home.

becoming the hostess with the mostest

Want to become the hostess with the mostest? While it may not happen overnight, there are a few things you can do to make the process easier.

1. Pray. Spend time with God and ask Him who you need to open your doors to. He'll be more than happy to show you!
2. Prioritize. Sometimes, we need to put stuff in its place by no longer prioritizing our clutter over the needs of others.
3. Prepare your home. Your home doesn't need to be Pinterest-perfect to have people over. Just clear off the dining table, order a pizza, and see what happens! Or do a 5-minute pickup of a small area like the entryway to help make your home feel more welcoming. #perfectionisoverrated
4. Probe the past. Study biblical examples to see how you can learn how to become the hostess with the mostest. Some New Testament passages you might want to read include Martha and her sister, Mary, in Luke 10 or John 12, as well as Lydia in Acts 16. In the Old Testament, there's the Shunammite Woman in 2 Kings 4, and Abraham and Sarah in Genesis 18.
5. Pull open the door and enjoy your company.

reflection:

What has kept you from inviting people into your home? How has that made you feel? How can this new mind shift make a difference?

Reflections

day 27
Two Different Perspectives

"But You, O Lord, are a shield for me, My glory and the One who lifts up my head."
Psalm 3:3 (NKJV)

Several years ago, I worked with a client I'll call "Ren," whose parents had died, leaving her the daunting task of clearing out their clutter-filled home and preparing it to sell. Ren apologized for the condition of the home. Everything she said about herself was also negative. Before I left, Ren said, "I don't suppose you'd want to come back, would you? ... Sorry I'm a difficult client."

"Of course I'll come back! You're a fantastic client." I smiled at her. "I want to help you finish this work. I also want to help you not speak negatively about yourself."

"Good luck with that," she said. "I've had a lot of practice."

Ren's reply saddened me. I don't know her well enough to know why she constantly berates herself. But I know the vision she has of herself is completely different from mine or God's.

I love the imagery of Psalm 3:3 and the way God gently transforms our thoughts with His Word.

As we scan the ever-present piles of clutter surrounding us, we may be tempted to bow our heads in shame, chastising ourselves yet again for our failure. "Why do I even try to get organized? I'm a helpless cause," and "I'll never change!"

But God lifts our head and declares, "Keep your eyes focused on Me, My dear child. I will supply everything you need. With My strength, you will have victory!"

Which voice will you listen to—your cries of condemnation that pull you further down into despair, or the voice of your Father, who knit you together with love and has always been your biggest fan?

God's perspective is the truest version of ourselves. We are who God says we are, not who we think we are or who others think we are. No matter how we feel about ourselves, we can choose to believe Him. And we can show this same love and acceptance to others, enabling them to see themselves as a recipient of God's love.

Angie

prayer

Day 27

Father, You've called me Your child, and You've demonstrated
Your unconditional love for me by sending Your Son.
Silence the enemy's lies and let me clearly hear Your voice.
I choose to believe what You say about me,
not what I believe about myself.
And I choose to see Your children as equally worthy
of that same unconditional love.

what god says about me

Sometimes we can be our own worst enemy. Our friends and family may try to build us up, yet we tear ourselves down. God's Word reminds us of His love and provision, but our negative thoughts cause us to doubt whether the words apply to us. We push ourselves in the opposite direction of where God is leading us, and we find ourselves floundering in a negative spiral.

We need to take God at His word and believe what He says about us. Remember, God's version is the truest version of ourselves. We are who God says we are, no matter how we feel.

- How I See Myself:

  ○ On a separate piece of paper, write down your common negative thoughts about yourself. What negative tapes play in your head? Don't hold back or sugarcoat them—get all of it down on paper, just like you experience it.

  ○ Now destroy that paper. You can rip it into pieces, shred it, burn it, or whatever you want to do. These thoughts are not serving you well, and you don't need them anymore. Your loved ones don't believe these things or speak to you that way.

More importantly, that's not how God speaks to you or sees you.

- How God Sees Me:

  ○ Now it's time to replace those lies with Truth. On the reflections page, record in your own words what God says about you in the following verses. These are just a few examples, but you can search for others. Put a star beside the ones that particularly apply to you, especially any that directly refute your negative thoughts.

    - 1 John 3:1
    - Psalm 103:1-12 (especially focus on v. 12)
    - Matthew 5:14-16
    - 1 Peter 2:9-10
    - John 15:13-15

Keep this list handy. You can use it when you're tempted to get back into that negative spiral. You may want to keep adding to this list over time.

Close your time in prayer, thanking God for His love and asking Him to help you see yourself the way He does.

reflection:

When negative thoughts about yourself come up again (and they will), how will you use what you've learned in this exercise to help you re-align with God's truth?

Reflections

day 28

Who Could You Be If You Were Clutter-Free?

"I have come that they may have life, and have it to the full."
John 10:10b (NIV)

"What would you do if you could do anything at all?" my sweet friend asked when I was at her house one morning. "If time, knowledge, or finances weren't issues, what's the one thing you'd want to accomplish?"

I gulped. I knew the answer to her loaded question. It would roll off my tongue as smooth as silk. But did I have the courage to state my dream out loud?

After several minutes of mentally hemming and hawing, I exhaled my response, "I'd write a novel."

Tilting her head, she smiled at me. "Then what's stopping you?"

"Nothing, really."

In that moment, it was true. There wasn't a single excuse I could offer for not writing a book like I'd dreamed about as a little girl. All I had to do was take that first step.

So, I did.

Shortly after that conversation, I pushed all other distractions aside and pursued my goal of becoming an author. Four and a half years later, I held *Perfectly Arranged,* the first book in my Hopeful Heart Series, in my hands.

All because someone was bold enough to ask a question that cut through my fears and doubts and encouraged me to see what might be possible.

Now I'd like to ask you a question. One that may force you to confront your deepest anxieties as well as allow you to live the full life Christ has called you to: Who could you be if you were clutter-free?

Maybe, like me, the answer is at the tip of your tongue, waiting for you to share it with the world. Or perhaps you need to give it some soul-searching thought. Take your time. Your answer may change your life forever, just as it did for me.

Whatever your response, remember—with God all things are possible. Place your heart's desire at His feet, and He will lift you up and give you the life you long for. It may not come right away or be easy, but you can rest assured He will guide your paths and make your ways straight. One could even say, clutter-free.

Liana

prayer

Lord, You came that I might have life and have it to the full.
I know that I've allowed my clutter to limit the abundant life
You offer, and I no longer want to be constrained
by its clutches.
Help me put aside all my fears and excuses
so I can be free to dream of who I could be
and who You've called me to be.
This is my heart's desire.

Now, Unclutter it!

20/20 vision

While God is the One who directs our steps, it can be fun to dream or imagine what our clutter-free future might look like. To help you get a 20/20 vision of that life, we want you to take some time and create a vision board.

1. Gather some magazines, poster board, scissors, glue, and markers.
2. Go through your collected materials and cut out images, words, and phrases that represent what your clutter-free life could look like. Be selective and choose items that evoke strong positive emotions.
3. Lay out the cutouts on your poster board without gluing them down initially. Experiment with different arrangements until you find a layout that feels right.
4. Once you're satisfied with the arrangement, glue down the cutouts. Be creative with the placement and overlapping of images.
5. Take a moment to step back and reflect on your vision board. Pray, visualize, and connect with the goals and dreams represented on the board.
6. Place your vision board in a prominent and easily visible location. Make sure you can see it regularly to reinforce your positive intentions.

reflection:

How did you feel creating the vision board? Hopeful? Excited? Journal your thoughts on your clutter-free life and determine what steps you need to take to make your dream a reality.

Reflections

now what?

Congratulations on reaching the end of the *Uncluttered* devotional! Now that you've made some strides in your journey to become uncluttered, you may be wondering where to go from here. We've got your back! The following are a few suggestions for your next steps:

1. **Check out our podcast.** Our podcast, which has the same title as this book, *Uncluttered: Shaping Your Heart & Home for What Matters Most*, is available on YouTube (bit.ly/3lnH55Z), Apple podcasts (apple.co/3Jnfh9Z), and every major podcast platform. In the show, we discuss additional topics related to organizing and faith, and interview Christian professional organizers and podcast listeners who have had success in uncluttering their lives.
2. **Visit our website, uncluttered.faith.** Our monthly blog includes inspiration and practical tips for decluttering and organizing. While you're there, subscribe to our newsletter and receive a free gift of decluttering signs. Our bimonthly updates let you know what's new on the podcast and offers helpful organizing tips.
3. **Find your focus.** Sometimes it can be helpful to choose one or two things you'd like to focus on at a time. Try

going back through this book and selecting a few topics. Work on these until you find success, then choose something else.

4. **Read through the devotionals and complete the exercises again.** Whether you do this right after you've gone through the book once or after a break, you'll probably notice some things you've missed, or you might be in a new season of life with a different mindset.

5. **Read Angie's book.** *Unholy Mess: What the Bible Says About Clutter* (https://amzn.to/3RwpMvE) is a faith-based book about decluttering and organizing, and it complements the *Uncluttered* material well. In addition, Angie's website (shipshape.solutions) contains numerous blogs and videos with decluttering and organizing tips.

6. **Listen to our Resource Roundup Episode.** You can find a list of our favorite organizing resources on our podcast— Season 1, Episode 11: Resource Roundup. You can also find a link to this resource list in the episode show notes on our website (bit.ly/3zN0Kjy).

7. **Add some accountability.** In Ephesians 4:9-10 and Proverbs 27:17, God's Word reminds us that we are better together. Find a person or group of people who can help you meet your goals, whether going through decluttering alongside you or just holding you accountable for the work.

8. **Hire a pro.** Sometimes the healthiest thing you can do is to bring in a professional. To find a professional organizer near you, go to the NAPO (National Association of Productivity and Organizing Professionals) website (napo.net). In the "Find a Pro" tab, enter your location to find someone to help you. Many organizers work virtually, which will give you more options. You can search specifically for a Christian professional organizer on the Faithful Organizers website (faithfulorganizers.com).

9. **Reach out to us.** We would love to hear from you and are here to help you! You can email us at

contact@uncluttered.faith and let us know your questions and your struggles. We're on your team!

Here's to becoming uncluttered together!

Liana and Angie

acknowledgments

from angie:

To Seana Turner: Thank you for mentioning me to Liana when she asked if you knew anyone who might be interested in learning about her fiction book series about a professional organizer. Who could have foreseen that our collaboration would lead to a friendship, a podcast, and a book? Clearly, God did, and He used *YOU* to do it.

To Christy Lynch and Brenda Tringali: Thank you for reading and commenting on so many pieces of this book as my workshopping partners. Your caring critique and friendship have been invaluable to me as a writer, and I'm so grateful for you.

To Linda Fulkerson and the staff of Scrivenings Press: Thank you for welcoming me into the Scrivenings Press family. I'm so honored to be a part of this wonderful team.

To Liana George: It's hard to put into words how much your friendship and our partnership has meant to me. I'm so humbled that you would work with me to create the Uncluttered podcast and to write this book. You've made me a better and more confident writer, and it's been such a joy to work with you.

To my husband Eric Hyche: You have stood beside me through every stage of my life, patiently assisting me in any way I needed. I couldn't ask for a more supportive husband. You are God's greatest gift on this earth to me, and I thank Him for you every day.

To my Heavenly Father: Thank you for giving me the skills and the passion to write and for connecting me to the people who would make this book a reality. I could fill many pages with all the ways you answered prayers about this book. My prayer for this book is that it would help others see You more clearly.

from liana:

I'm so grateful to have the opportunity to write this book, but I know it wouldn't have been possible without the following:

To my wonderful Scrivenings Press family, thank you for taking a chance on this idea and making it a reality.

To Seana Turner, for connecting me with Angie. Who knew what would bloom from a simple introduction? Thank you so much.

To my ever-faithful writing support team (you know who you are), your prayers and encouragement carried me once more on this writing project.

To my friend, co-host, and co-author, Angie, I appreciate you partnering with me on this *Uncluttered* journey. I know it has been a roller coaster ride over the last three years and I appreciate your patience with me. It has been a pleasure and an honor to work with you.

To my family for always believing in me and supporting me. I love you more!

And finally to God, for whom this book would not exist. You planted the seed of this devotion in my heart so long ago and waited patiently for me to get my act together. Then You divinely brought Angie into my life and allowed the seed to grow. May the fruit of this book and those it reaches bring You honor and glory.

about liana george

Liana George considers herself a multipotentialite—a person with many interests and creative pursuits. Because of her status as such, Liana took the long, winding road to becoming an author. Not because she never wanted to write (because she did!), but because there were so many other things she wanted to try first, such as teaching, running children's programs at the churches she attended, and helping people declutter and organize their lives.

When marriage and motherhood collided at the intersection of the road she traveled, the journey toward authorship took even longer. But Liana never gave up on her childhood dreams and at the age of 50 signed her first book contract for her debut novel *Perfectly Arranged* with Scrivenings Press. With three novels under her belt, Liana's brain is filled with stories to share and she can't write fast enough to get them all down on paper (yes, she handwrites all her books).

When she isn't busy scribbling away, Liana enjoys spending time with her husband of 30 years, Clint, on their small farm on the outskirts of Houston, Texas, guiding her two daughters, Kayley and Abbey, into adulthood, watching tennis, reading, or planning her next beach and dive vacation.

about angie hyche

Angie Hyche is a certified professional organizer (CPO®), author, speaker, and the owner of Shipshape Solutions. She is passionate about helping her readers and listeners declutter and simplify their lives so they can focus on what's most important and spend time doing what they love.

Angie and her husband Eric live in a small downtown loft in Kingsport, Tennessee. In 2019, they were thrilled to shed approximately 75% of their belongings in order to move into the small space and to simplify their lives. This experience, as well as her seven years working in client homes and businesses, has provided motivation to help others see the consequences of clutter.

Her first book, *Unholy Mess: What the Bible Says about Clutter,* was published on Amazon in December of 2020. In the book, she shares how her experiences working with clients and her own life experiences helped her see the far-reaching consequences of clutter. She learned that clutter goes much deeper and broader than just physical belongings. Angie openly shares her personal journey of clearing her schedule clutter (a packed calendar and to-do list) and attention clutter (smartphone addiction and a lack of focus).

When she's not organizing or writing, you'll find Angie on a hiking or bicycle trail with her husband, visiting her adult daughters Emma and Lydia, reading, or performing in community theatre.

also by angie hyche

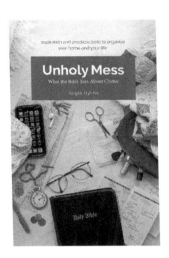

Do you feel empty even though your life is full?

Have you lost the ability to focus on what really matters because your home, your schedule, and your mind are cluttered with the insignificant? Do you long for a deeper relationship with God that isn't crowded out by the unholy mess you've accumulated? Then this book is exactly what you need. *Unholy Mess* will:

- **Open your eyes** to the pervasiveness of clutter and its far-reaching effects.
- Encourage you to examine how your clutter is holding you back from the **peaceful and focused Christian life** you desire.
- Provide inspiration from Scripture for a healthy relationship with your possessions and **a deeper relationship with God.**
- Share stories of the **freedom** that comes from letting go.
- Give you practical steps to overcome the obstacles, organize your home, and **maintain the order.**

Reading *Unholy Mess* will empower you to find the simplicity that lies beneath the clutter, to rekindle your passion for God, and to enjoy a peaceful and ordered life.

Get your copy at Amazon:

amazon.com/Unholy-Mess-Bible-About-Clutter/dp/1734959797

also by liana george

Perfectly Arranged

Book One of the Hopeful Hearts series

Short on clients and money, professional organizer Nicki Mayfield is hanging up her label maker. That is until the eccentric socialite Katherine O'Connor offers Nicki one last job.

Working together, the pair discovers an unusual business card among Ms. O'Connor's family belongings that leads them on a journey to China. There the women embark on an adventure of faith and self-discovery as they uncover secrets, truths, and ultimately, God's perfectly arranged plans.

Get your copy here:

https://scrivenings.link/perfectlyarranged

Perfectly Placed

Book Two of the Hopeful Hearts series

Six weeks after leaving China, Nicki Mayfield returns to complete two critical tasks: restore order at New Hope Orphanage and re-connect with the little girl who stole her heart. However, between a stubbornly stone walling supervisor, missing documents, and personal tragedy, Nicki faces challenges at every turn. Is she the best person to bring order – and longevity – to the place these children call home?

Then, with the help of an unexpected ally, Nicki makes a life-altering decision that upends her well-planned life and the lives of those around her. Will she lose it all, or has she found the way to save what matters most?

Get your copy here:

https://scrivenings.link/perfectlyplaced

Perfectly Matched

Book Three of the Hopeful Hearts series

Nicki Mayfield is getting married!

Or is she?

Three days after deciding to marry so she can adopt the young Chinese girl who has captured her heart, Nicki Mayfield heads to Texas to become Mrs. Ben Carrington. However, as the unlikely pair prepares to say, "I do," a shocking revelation threatens their plans to become a family.

While searching for the answers to the mystery holding her future hostage, Nicki must also keep Ms. O'Connor's legacy alive at New Hope Orphanage – whose future is at serious risk.

As she and Ben work toward building their unconventional family, they discover that sacrificial parenting requires putting the child first in ways that bring indescribable joy and unexpected heartbreak to everyone involved.

In the end, will Nicki find her happily ever after or will circumstances stop her from being perfectly matched in work, life, and love?

Get your copy here:

https://scrivenings.link/perfectlymatched

Stay up-to-date on your favorite books and authors with our free e-newsletters.

ScriveningsPress.com

Made in the USA
Columbia, SC
13 May 2024

35278412R00137